THE CAMBRIA
STORY

GW00390899

—— R O B E R T   S I M P E R ——

THE CAMBRIA
STORY

PUBLISHED 2012 by Creekside Publishing

Printed by Lavenham Press
ISBN 978-0-9563299-2-9

CONTENTS

Acknowledgements   04

The Edwardian Barge Boom   06

Famous Coasting Barge   12

Into the Second Century   31

Principle Details   55

Source of Illustrations   55

Thanks to William Everard for the background to the Everard family's shipping firm. Details of the loss of the *Hibernia* came from Harry Couchman, grandson of the skipper, living in Tasmania. Local information came from Rene Waite, the historian of Pin Mill, and details of Margate from Mick Twyman. Philip 'Ginger' Latham, Tony Farnham and Robert Daws gave their memories of sailing with Bob Roberts. Barry Peace made his first barging trip on *Cambria* and provided much useful information to help compile this story. Tony Winter for the barge's final years of trading. Tim Goldsack, master shipwright and barge restorer, gave details of the rebuild. The Cambria Trust took on the Maritime Trust's material that included the 'Story of the Cambria' booklet. This has much information that had got lost in the intervening years.

It is likely that the *Cambria* is the most photographed of all the spritsail sailing barges, but it was still difficult to get enough photographs. I am grateful to Richard Walsh, editor of *Tops'l*, for two photographs of the barge sailing in 1969, which came from the Beazley Collection in the SSBR archives. When Patricia O'Driscoll was mate on the barges, between 1958-70, she recorded many events with her camera and she has lent some of the *Cambria* taken between 1959-1964.

Project manager William Collard collected many details of *Cambria's* history during the restoration and passed them and photographs on to be incorporated into the *Cambria's* long story. My wife Pearl and I took several of the other photographs. The identity of other photographers has been lost in the mist of time and we are sorry we can't record them.

RS
Ramsholt 2012

Left: The *Cambria's* skipper Nobby Finch, after a Thames Match in the 1930s.

Miss Alice Ethel Everard, with the Everard family, launching the *Cambria* at Greenhithe, 1906.

The *Cambria's* sister ship *Hibernia* passing Pin Mill.

The sailing barge *Cambria* is a fast, handy and attractive spritsail barge, one of the finest of her type ever built. When she was launched in 1906 the sailing barges were at their peak, with over two thousand of them trading, mostly from ports around the Thames Estuary. Barges had been slowly evolving over the past hundred and fifty years so that a great deal of trial and error had gone before her.

In nautical circles the sailing barge *Cambria* and her last trading skipper Bob Roberts, became famous on the East Coast and beyond. I had heard of A.W. 'Bob' Roberts long before I saw the *Cambria*. Bob Roberts barge book the *'Coasting Bargemaster'* was published in 1949. This is a breezy well-written account of how Bob, a young man from Dorset first went to sea. In the 1920s Bob came up to the East Coast because the barges were still trading under sail alone while most of the remaining West Country schooners and ketches were fitted with auxiliary engines. Bob was a hard working young man capable of skippering a barge.

When Bob Roberts joined the firm run by Will and Fred Everard they were rapidly expanding their fleet of coastal vessels. This fleet was based at Greenhithe, by the Thames in north Kent. Although concentrating on modern vessels F. T. Everard & Sons still had a fleet of sailing barges including the *Martinet*, the last of the 'boomie' barges. The 95ft boomie *Martinet* was built at Rye in 1912, and loaded 210 tons.

The boomie barges had flat bottoms and needed leeboards in order to sail against the wind, but while spritsail barges only needed two men (and sometimes a boy) to handle their sails, the boomies with their heavy booms and gaff sails needed three or four strong men. The barge crews were paid on a share of the cargo money. The more men aboard the less money there was to go around at the end of the trip.

Many skippers were reluctant to take on the *Martinet* so the Everard's were very glad when they found a young chap, Bob Roberts, with experience in Westcountry gaff schooners, who was willing to take on the last boomie. Before becoming skipper of *Martinet*, Bob had also worked as a journalist for the *Daily Mail* and had done some ocean voyages in yachts.

In spite of his time in gaff sailed schooners Bob had got used to the 'easier to handle' spritsail rig and disliked the *Martinet's* hand-spike windlass. He called her the 'wicked old' *Martinet*, but was skipper of the barge until she sank, loaded with cement, in Hollesley Bay in 1941. The barge's cargoes were vital to the war effort, but under wartime regulations no craft on its own was allowed to be 'under way' at night and had to anchor where ever they were. Sailing barges could not regulate their speed and the *Martinet* was forced to anchor in Hollesley Bay. During the night the wind got up, the barge rolled and started to leak badly and a wave smashed her boat. The crew fired flares, which were luckily seen from the shore, and just as the crew of the *Martinet* began to think there was no hope, the Aldeburgh lifeboat arrived and took them off.

Bob Roberts did not say exactly where the *Martinet* sank, but Felixstowe Ferry fishermen, who trawl in Hollesley Bay, say that there is a lump of concrete inside the Whiting Bank near the Hook Buoy. This would appear to have been a reasonably sheltered spot for a barge to anchor for the night.

Once ashore Bob Roberts travelled to Great Yarmouth and took on being skipper of Everard's steel spritsail rigged barge *Greenhithe* and he stayed with her until she was scrapped. After a spell ashore, at his old calling of journalism, he became skipper of Everard's wooden spritsail barge *Cambria* in 1954 and remained with her for the next sixteen years.

In 1960 Bob Roberts published his book '*Last of the Sailormen*,' by which time he was skipper of two barges; the *Cambria* for working and he raced *Dreadnought*, which was owned by a subsidiary of Everards. In this book he is very definitely summing up what he believed to be the end of the sailing barges and indeed his own career, but he had a long way to go and

barges are still sailing.

The man responsible for the *Cambria's* creation was Frederick Thomas Eberhardt (This German name was changed to Everard in World War I.) F. T. Everard started off working as a shipwright for the barge builder Keep, at Battersea. Alfred Keep then moved to Greenhithe, on the lower Thames in north Kent. F. T. Everard also moved to Greenhithe with Keep. Some say that he pushed his tools there in a hand barrow and others that he walked there with his tools on his back. Which ever way it was, it became the beginning of F. T. Everard's a very successful business association with Alfred and then Harry Keep.

The Keeps, and the shipwright Everard, were very much involved in a period of expansion and experimentation with barges. In 1874 Alfred Keep built the 114ft schooner barge *Greenhithe*. Everard was clearly getting more involved in the business side and bought the thirty-year-old small barge *Industry* to trade. In 1898 F. T. Everard built his first barge under his own name, the *Doffoly*, with Harry Keep being the first managing owner. The second barge they built at Greenhithe, the *Lord Kitchener*, was in 1899, and she later appeared on the register as being owned by F. T. Everard. They built more sailing barges, the *Britisher* and *Anglo American* in 1902, both appear as being built for F. T. Everard. The *Lady Maud* was built for Johnson Cement Works in 1903 and the same year the big coasting barge *Scotia*, which was very similar to the later *Cambria*, but had no wheel-shelter. The *Scotia* was registered as being owned by F. T. Everard, and was eventually lost off Great Yarmouth.

F.T. Everard had sent his two sons, Fred and Will, to be apprentices at Fellows, the Great Yarmouth ship builders. When they returned to Greenhithe he said they must each build a barge and keep accounts to see who could do it for the least cost. These barges became the last two designed by F T Everard. This was a good discipline for the two young men starting out in

Horlock's *Reminder* and Everard's *Cambria* racing in the Thames in about 1934.

the barge building trade. Using trees cut down in Kent, Will built the 91ft 'Welsh' barge *Cambria* for £1,895, and Fred built the 'Irish' barge *Hibernia* for £1,905, only a £10 difference. In 1906 the two barges were launched on the same day.

When seen under sail it was very difficult to tell these two Everard coasting barges apart. Bargemen called them 'mulie' rigged because they had the gaff mizzen of the Victorian boomies, but had the spritsail rig on the mainmast. There were already many steamers in the coasting trade, but they were expensive to operate and the sailing barges still had little trouble in under-cutting their freights to the smaller ports.

The *Cambria* appeared on the register as being built for W. Eberhardt (Everard), but the following year she was sold to Harry Keep and

at the same time half the sixty-four shares of *Hibernia* were also sold to Keep. This sounds like a cash flow problem because they both came back under Everard's ownership later. In about 1910 there was a trade slump and Goldsmiths of Grays managed to get Keep's work carrying coal to Margate and Broadstairs. Keep then auctioned off some of his barges at Gravesend and at the same time Everard bought up several barges and then concentrated on his barge owning operation.

In 1913 the Everards launched their auxiliary boom sail barge *Grit*, at the Greenhithe yard. She was sunk by German submarine fire in 1916. This vessel was replaced with another *Grit*, a motor ship, which was built in 1921, and she was sunk in a collision off Hythe in 1934. Both these *Grits* looked very similar to *Cambria*.

Every tide saw fleets of barges going up and

down the Thames in front of Greenhithe. The *Cambria* and *Hibernia* were some of the finest on the tideway, but there was nothing unusual about them when they first appeared on the Thames. There were well over two thousands Thames sailing barges, of many different types, trading all around the English coast, and many went to Scotland and Ireland as well, and to the near Continentals ports. There was a tremendous variety of barges, from the little 'stumpie' barges that carried cement and bricks to build London, up to coasters, such as *Cambria*, that took freights where they were fixed.

The *Cambria* was a good 'earner' for her owners and crew as she loaded 170

'Cully' Tovell of Pin Mill at the wheel of the *Cambria* in 1940

tons, or seventeen railway truck loads of coal. She also carried cargoes to Antwerp, Dunkirk, Calais and Treport. This type of load put her deck amidships down to just 11.5 inches above the water. The crew of three, skipper, mate and third hand, usually a boy to do the cooking, could set 5,000 sq. ft. of sail. By the standard of the day the skipper's panelled cabin aft was very impressive. There was also a spare bunk in the aft cabin while the mate and third hand, lived forward in the fo'c'sle where the cooking was done on a coal burning stove. It varied from barge to barge, but usually the food was taken down to the skipper in his cabin.

Although they were supposed to be sister barges, the *Cambria* was always faster than the *Hibernia*. The *Cambria's* first skipper was 24-year-old Ernest Francis Milton; better known to his fellow bargemen as 'Brusher.' He had been born in 1882 and had worked on barges since

he was fourteen and at twenty became a skipper with Everards.

He took his wife away on some trips in the summer and in 1909 she went with him when the *Cambria* took cement to Deauville to build the casino. In 1912 the Milton's six week old daughter went with them on a trip, and slept in a drawer as a cot. The Miltons settled at Lennox Road, Gravesend and on the walls of their house Brusher Milton proudly displayed pictures of the Everard barges that he had sailed on.

Once Brusher Milton left the Solent at the same time as a steamer, which was capable of making nine knots, but she could not keep up with the *Cambria* that arrived at Dover first. Back in the office the Everard Brothers loved to hear accounts like this and expected their skippers to 'crack on' and make fast passages. When she beat the steamer Brusher Milton, had set a mizzen tops'l, a staysail on the mizzen mast and even hoisted the sail on the barge's boat in the davits!

Carrying cargoes on the open coast of Britain in a small wooden sailing barge was a hard life and at time, dangerous. In 1913 on January 19 the Spurn Head lifeboat went off to assist the *Cambria*. In 1920 the barge is recorded as trading from London to the French ports under Captain Milton and on February 24 the Dungeness lifeboat assisted the barge in heavy weather.

Because of *Cambria's* reputation for making smart passages Everards entered her in the Thames and Medway Sailing Barge Matches in

Mate and Third Hand of the *Cambria* hauling on the mains'l sheet, 1940.

1927. Everards also entered their two new steel barges, *Ethel Everard* and *Fred Everard*, that could (before engines were fitted) load 300tons. These were, with their later sisters *Alf Everard* and *Will Everard* the largest spritsail barges ever built. Annual barge races were held at several ports around the Thames Estuary in the Victorian period and the Thames and Medway races were the most prestigious and were reported in the London newspapers. When the Thames and Medway races were revived after World War I, the Everard family followed the races on the committee steamers and were well aware of the publicity a win brought to their growing firm. The *Cambria*, with her smartly painted white stern, went on to be a regular prizewinner in the inter-war races.

Everards were busy building up their fleet of coastal traders and one of the ways to do this was to get regular contracts so that their vessels were never waiting for the next freight. The Everards got contracts to supply the gas works, around the Thames Estuary, with coal from the Humber ports. In 1927 the *Cambria* and *Hibernia*, with Everards coasting barges *Will Everard*, *Alf Everard*, *Royalty*, *Martinet*, *Britisher* and *Greenhithe* regularly took coal to Margate gas works. The 97ft *Will Everard* once sailed with coal from Keadby from the Humber to Margate in 30 hours.

On Sept 1 1940 *Cambria* loaded 128tons of coke at Rochester for discharge at Margate. However for some of World War II Margate was closed as a port and when it reopened in 1945 the *Cambria* and *Will Everard* took some freights before the gas works closed in May 1958.

In October 25, 1937 the *Hibernia* loaded 154tons of coal at Goole for the gas works at Sittingbourne. Unfortunately a series of heavy gales swept across the North Sea and the *Hibenria* lay 'windbound' in Grimsby Roads for two weeks. Finally skipper Harry Couchman judged that the weather had changed and he heaved up his anchor and began a passage down the North Sea.

The wind remained moderate for sometime, but then very heavy squalls started coming in from the North-East. The barge was trapped on a lee shore. She could not go back and shelter in the Humber or make the shelter of Yarmouth Roads, way off to the south. On November 9 at 3pm Couchman and his young crew, found the barge was taking in water. The fo'c'sle, where the crew lived, had four feet of water in it. For five hours Harry Couchman, his sixteen-year-old son and eighteen-year-old mate William Tate continued to work the hand pumps, while heavy seas swept over the deeply laden barge.

Once a steamer came up to the *Hibernia*, but in those seas she could not render any assistance. The steamer radioed the Happisburgh Light Vessel, who in turn got in touch with the Cromer RNLI station. No one was quite certain where the sinking barge was, her sails had blown away and the crew had fired their last two distress rockets. They had given up any hope of saving the barge and their fate didn't look good.

However coxswain Henry Blogg had launched the Cromer lifeboat and was attempting to find out where the barge was by radio. At 9.45pm they sighted the barge, now completely awash and at 10pm they went alongside in the dark and took the three men off, one by one. They were exhausted and soaked to the skin. The barge remained afloat with her sails all torn. A newspaper report said that she 'swept past Cromer like a phantom ship, with only one light showing.'

At 3pm she was driven ashore at Runton, a mile and half past Cromer. Over the years several barges had been driven ashore there. The previous autumn the *Lady Gwynfred* had been ashore there for several weeks, but *Hibernia* was not so lucky as she broke in two and the forward end remained standing upright with Everard's famous red and white 'bob' house flag flying at the mainmast head.

Ashore, skipper Harry 'Uncle Fred' Couchman of Greenhithe said the old ship had let him down, but praised his crew. A newspaper cutting showed William Lane and Harry Couchman of Greenhithe, mate and third hand of the *Hibernia*, enjoying a meal of fish and chips at Gorleston after being rescued.

The *Cambria* and *Scotia* laden with coal at Keadby on the River Trent in about 1935. Because of the strong tide the barges were normally towed up from Hull.

During World War II Frank 'Cully' Tovell, from Pin Mill, in Suffolk, skippered the *Cambria*. According to a newspaper cutting of 1940 'Cully' had been at sea for forty-two years and had been a barge master in the coasting trade of thirty-three of these years. The barge, with two young teenage boys as crew, was making coasting passages unarmed and didn't sail in convoys. A photo, in a newspaper cutting, shows Cully in the master's stern cabin listening to the midnight news on his radio under the light from an oil cabin lamp. Perhaps because of this report Cully was asked by the BBC to go up to London and record some of his experiences in barges.

Cambria's fame as a celebrity barge had begun rather quietly, but the publicity around her grew as the decades went by. At the end of World War II, most of the coasting barges had been fitted with engines, but Everards still had three sailing barges in the coasting trade, the *Greenhithe*, *Will Everard* and *Cambria*. The *Greenhithe* was scrapped and the *Will Everard* was fitted with an engine so that in 1948 Roger Finch, writing in *Sea Breezes*, describes *Cambria* 'as being the last sailing barge to visit Norwich,' In fact she went on making visits to Norwich with wheat over the next twenty years, but it was the first time someone used the term 'last' in connection with *Cambria* and it was probably the beginning of her fame as the 'last sailing barge.'

The *Will Everard*, with an engine and sails, went on carrying cargoes for another sixteen years. Although the *Will Everard* was a good earner for the company, she was never a handy sailor. As the engine fitted was not powerful enough to make her solely a motor vessel she always used sails and engine at sea. Once when the *Thyra* and *Will Everard* were caught in a gale on passage 'sailing light' from the Humber to the Wash the *Thyra* was able to get into Boston while the high sided *Will Everard* was blow off along the Norfolk coast and had to anchor off

Skipper Billy Standard of Southwold in *Cambria's* stern cabin, 1954.

Cromer and wait for calm weather to get to King's Lynn.

In the winter the *Cambria* was trading to Ipswich, Norwich and Yarmouth, but, if called on, she still took part in the coal trade from Keadby to Harwich gas works. Keadby is a village on the River Trent that Bob Roberts, in his breezy way, describes as 'a row of cottages, three pubs and a coal chute.' In fact it was a bit more than that because it was at the end of a railway line and the Stainforth and Keadby Canal that made it a major outlet for the East Midlands coal fields.

In January 1952 the *Cambria* was discharging flour at Lowestoft, which means that the Everards must have had great confidence in her to send a wooden barge nearly fifty years old up the coast in mid-winter with a highly perishable cargo. There were still about twenty barges

The *Cambria* sailing light out of Whitstable harbour, on November 4 1963.

carrying cargoes under sail in the Thames Estuary, but by this time only the *Cambria* was carrying cargoes under sail past Orfordness into the North Sea.

In 1954 Frank 'Cully' Tovell had to retire as skipper of the *Cambria* and 46-year-old Ernest William Stannard of Southwold took over. Ernie Stannard was later reported in a newspaper as saying that the 118 tons of cargo of cottonseed he loaded in London was the first time the barge had been to Hull since before World War II. As the barge approached the Humber she was hit by a west-north-westerly gale. The jib carried away and shortly afterwards the half mains'l split 'like a burst of a gun.' Captain Stannard and his mate William Evans went without sleep for the next thirty-six hours.

The weather had slightly improved when they finally got the barge into the Humber, under fores'l and mizzen, and slowly made their way up to Hull and along side Alexandra Quay to discharge. The barge then returned to the Thames and Stannard left.

Everards wrote to Bob Roberts and offered him the barge. After the *Martinet*, Bob had taken on the spritsail 'mulie' barge *Greenhithe* in the coasting trade as far north as Keadby, on the River Trent. In 1949 at fifteen years old Tony Farnham joined Bob Roberts as third hand on the *Greenhithe*. Tony had grown up on the Greenhithe waterfront and knew all the men on Everard's barges. Tony and the mate of the *Greenhithe* lived forward in the fo'c'sle while Bob Roberts lived and ate alone in the aft cabin.

Tony Farnham said Bob Roberts would only explain something once, and after that if you got it wrong he shouted at you. Bob's way of waking up his young mate and third hand was to open the fo'c'sle scuttle and throw wooden hatch wedges at them in their bunks. After nine

The charter barge *Will* of Maldon, formerly the trading barge *Will Everard* of London, entering Brightlingsea in 2007. Like the *Cambria* this barge was called a 'mulie' because she had a gaff mizzen and spritsail mains'l. While Everards mostly kept the *Cambria* on the Yarmouth and Norwich run the *Will Everard* went to many ports such as Hull, Lynn, Wells and Whitstable.

months, Tony decided to leave the *Greenhithe* and joined Cully on the *Cambria*.

To get away from the bombing, during World War II, Bob Roberts moved his wife and two daughters from Bexley, near Greenhithe, to Pin Mill on the River Orwell. Pin Mill is the riverside part of Chelmondiston. Behind the Green is a little group of cottages beside a narrow footpath. The hamlet had long been the home of bargemen and watermen. It was a place that Bob Roberts fitted into well, particularly the 'Butt and Oyster,' at the top of Pin Mill landing hard, which was a short walk from his home.

Even under sail a barge master in the coasting trade was still earning a good income. In August 1949 the Dwiny Cottage, half way up the group of cottages near the Grindle stream, was purchased by the Roberts from the University of Oxford that was selling up its estate at Chelmondiston. The cottage was mortgaged for £2,000 in the name of Amelia Roberts. In 1959 Bob Roberts and a neighbour purchased the meadow, behind the cottages, from the University of Oxford. The Roberts sold the property in 1973 for £10,000, of which £3,000 went to Bob Roberts.

The *Greenhithe* traded up the coast to Keadby

aboard the *Cambria* and became her skipper. In one of his books '*Last of the Sailormen*' Bob Roberts said of the *Cambria* 'for me it was pleasant to tread a wooden deck again. I decided she was the best and most comfortable ship I had been in, with the possible exception of the boom-rigged *Martinet*.'

When Bob joined the *Cambria*, the mate was Bill Evans, a silent, likeable man who had already been on the barge eight years. He had stayed for another three years before getting married and taking a job ashore. The third hand was fifteen-year-old Nobby Larkin, a bargeman's son from Gillingham. Two year later I met Nobby on the *Will Everard* and he spoke with great affection about Bob and Bill, but as he wanted to go further afield he joined the *Will Everard* that was then trading any where between Exeter and Hull. The *Will Everard's* skipper was skipper Paddy O'Donnell, a fisherman from Northern Ireland who had been cook, third hand and mate on the *Will Everard* before becoming master of one Everard's motor coasters. When skipper Jim Uglow left the *Will Everard*, the company told Paddy that he was only man they had to take on the barge.

As the *Will Everard* only had a low powered engine she couldn't push against a head sea and had to be sailed all the time. The barge by this stage only set a main, tops'l and fores'l. At Greenhithe Everards had a great store of old barge sails and as the *Will's* sail blew away another one was dispatched as a replacement. Under a hard working and capable skipper, like Paddy, the auxiliary barge, loading about 280tons, must still have been a 'good earner' for Everards and they kept her trading until 1966.

Bob and Paddy, skippers of Everard's remaining two active sailing barges, were great friends, but very different people. Paddy regarded his barge as being 'Nelson's Patent' and returned to command one of Everards motor ships running to the Isle of Wight and later moved to the Island. Bob loudly decried motor vessels and plugged on with sail to the bitter end.

When Nobby joined the *Will Everard* seventeen-year-old Cyril Wright was third hand, but soon

for coal for the gas works and took cattle food to Great Yarmouth. When the barge failed her survey Everards offered Bob one of their modern motor coasters, but he was determined to stay in sail or quit the sea. Bob decided to get a job near his home at Pin Mill and for three years, was a sub-editor on the *East Anglian Daily Times* in Ipswich. He bought the Whitstable smack *Stormy Petrel*, that didn't have an engine, and tried his hand at trawling under sail at weekends. By this stage he had written two books and was becoming well known as a folk singer.

On October 29, 1954 Bob Roberts stepped

became mate. In October 1955 the *Will Everard* was returning from the Isle of Wight when she was hit by a gale. The sails, which were in a fairly poor state, blew away and the engine broke down. In heavy seas they anchored near Dungeness and fired distress rockets. The Dungeness lifeboat came out and took Paddy, Cyril and Nobby off. The barge then dragged out into the English Channel.

Next day the French fishing boat *Jacues Henri* found the barge drifting and went alongside, but in the heavy seas the steel barge smashed the wooden fishing boat and she sank, the fishermen leapt on to the barge as their craft went down behind them. Later the same day another French boat, the *Marie Rose Robert*, found the barge and towed her into Dieppe. Here the French placed an armed guard aboard to prevent the barge from being taken before salvage was paid. The ancient rivalry between the two sides of the Channel was still very much alive then.

Bob Roberts, Skipper-owner of the barge *Cambria*

When the *Will Everard's* crew returned their first job was to remove the huge French flag flying from the mizzen. The barge was loaded with apples (Everards were not going to miss a freight back) and set off for Everard's shipyard at Greenhithe. Unfortunately it was thick fog in the Channel and all Paddy O'Donnell had to navigate with was a large-scale chart and compass. Standing in the wheelhouse in the dark, with fog so thick they couldn't see the bow, Paddy admitted to Cyril that they were lost and shortly afterwards they ploughed up on Dungeness beach.

Again the Dungeness lifeboat came out to them and one lifeboatman said 'not you again!' and asked Cyril for the jacket back that he had lent him a few weeks before. None of these adventures put Nobby off barging and at seventeen he returned to *Cambria* as mate, taking Bill Evans place.

Barge owners really liked it when their skippers made fast passages and in 1956 Bob Roberts did just that with *Cambria*. From Yarmouth to Southend, light in twelve hours and then deeply laden from Greenhithe to Yarmouth in seventeen hours. There were still over twenty barges trading under sail, although some were Woods 'power barges' that were often towed about the Thames. Only the *Cambria* was still

The *Cambria* in the Surrey Commercial Docks loading 144 tons of ground nut extract for Bunns, Great Yarmouth, March, 1959

still taking coal from Keadby regularly, to the gas works at Harwich and Colchester.

The *Cambria* had been built for the general coastal trade, but in the mid-twentieth century she became the very last sailing collier and then took imported foodstuffs from the London Docks to East Coast mills.

In 1955 Bob skippered the *Cambria*, which had not raced since 1938, in the Thames and Medway races. However the coaster *Cambria*, with her working sails, was no match for the smaller racing barges. The Everard Brothers decided to drag the hulk of the *Veronica* off the foreshore and fit her out to race again.

Will and Fred Everard were largely responsible for reviving the two annual working barge races. In 1953 to celebrate the Coronation of Queen Elizabeth II it was decided to hold the 'very last barge race' in the Thames. After this the Thames and then Medway Races were restarted. The publicity from winning races had made good commercial sense, and the Everard brothers had lost none of their desire to win. They increased the sail plan of *Sara* and *Veronica* appeared under a massive sail and then, under a subsidiary firm, the *Dreadnought*, was also fitted out just to take part in the races. While their rival, the London & Rochester Trading Company, later Crescent Shipping of Strood, fitted out their barge *Sirdar*. Other private owners were later allowed to join in to keep the races going.

These 'revival' races were such a success that they triggered off a renewed interest in sailing barges. Everards and Crescent Shipping, kept

making some runs to the Humber, for coal from Keadby, but these were getting less frequent. Although in 1957 she took coal to Margate from Keadby.

For over four hundred years sailing ships had brought coal down the coast to ports in East and Southern England. In the mid-nineteenth century it was not unusual to see a fleet of a hundred or more collier brigs pass through Yarmouth Roads in a day. Even in the 1890s Ernest Cooper, Town Clerk of Southwold, counted 110 sailing colliers sheltering in Sole Bay in a North Westerly gale. Railways gradually took the coal trade away, but Everards negotiated contracts to supply many East Coast gas works by sea. In 1957 the *Will Everard* was

The *Cambria* alongside lighters, ready to lock out of the Albert Basin in April, 1961. She had loaded 713quarters of wheat in bulk at the Victoria Dock for Marriage's Mill at Felixstowe Dock

The *Cambria* seen from the barge *Edith Maud* in the Lower Hope in February, 1962

barges just to take part in these two races. Because they were not carrying cargoes the new Champion Class barges were given a huge spread of canvas, pushing the flat-bottomed spritsail barges to their limits in speed. In the final Thames race in 1963 the *Veronica* won at an average speed of 10.309 knots around the course, and in the smooth water coming up to the finish she was recorded doing fourteen knots.

However the hulls of some of the Champion Class barges were held together with wire stays and the barges had lost all the easy handling qualities of the spritsail rig. After ten years the two companies agreed to stop racing, because of the expense. To keep the old style barges racing going Everards had to fit out three barges and then crews spent a week sailing to get them up to speed for just two race days. The real expense had been that the racing skippers would not have young bargemen, but insisted on taking their former bargemen friends as race crews. Since most of these men were then masters and mates of Everard's coasters it meant that this almost brought the company to a standstill. One year Everards had ten ships laid up while their masters were away racing the barges.

The abandonment of the Thames and Medway Races (which have since been restarted) was also intended to be an official ending of the sailing barge era and Everards decided to break up all their Champion barges.

This was a real tragedy because the *Sara* and *Dreadnought* were broken up the following year and their gear sold for *Edith May* and *Dawn*. The *Veronica*, one of the fastest and most attractive barges ever built, never sailed again. Everards sold *Veronica*, insisting that she could not use that name again. She became a houseboat under the name *Veronica Belle* at Rochester and in 1976 her hulk was dumped in Bedlams Bottom, Funton Creek on the River Medway.

Bob Roberts greatly approved that the famous barges were taken out of commission. In his logic it was better for these beautiful barges

The *Olive May* had towed the *Cambria* down to the lock gates at Tilbury, January 28, 1963. As they were near the open sea Bob Roberts was getting the bowsprit down. On the left is the mate Vernon Parker who had been on the barge for a year and didn't know how much longer he would be there. The barge had loaded at Tilbury with a split cargo for Great Yarmouth, 50tons of cotton seed cake for Lee Barber and 100tons of ground nut extract for Bunns

to be destroyed than for them to be sailed by 'some half-baked romantics.' Bob had no time for people who sailed barges for pleasure and equally bitterly hated the new use of sailing barges, which has been instrumental in keeping them going, as 'charter barges' carrying passengers.

However, it was good news for the *Cambria* because with the expenses of the Champion Class barges over, Everards decided to give the *Cambria* a major refit the following year. Luckily for *Cambria* (she does appear to have always been a lucky barge, as well as a handsome one) she returned to Everard's wharf at Greenhithe and was re-fastened and her sides doubled with another layer of planks. The transom was 'doubled' (a layer of planks over the original stern) and the name and port of registration re-carved on the new stern, but this was lower down than the original name which had the *C* of *Cambria* and the L of London carved slightly higher than the other letters, a trademark Everards used on the other barges they had

The *Cambria*, turning down the River Medway, after discharging 2000bags of asbestos at Barnetts Wharf, Strood. March 9, 1964

built.

When writing about these years, Bob Roberts said that Will Everard had a soft spot for the *Cambria*, the barge he had built as a young man, and when ever Bob asked him for anything to be repaired it was always done so that the barge was in 'better nick' than the others still trading.. Most barges had pitch pine planking 'rabbetted', but Will Everard had built the *Cambria* with each plank overlapping half the next one, which made her very strong. Wooden spritsail barges had been built for over a century and when *Cambria* was built they were getting it down to a fine art. Her hull used a massive amount of timber, but this was done very economically. Sadly in 1958, two days after the Medway race, Will Everard, builder of the *Cambria*, died suddenly.

The *Cambria* is remembered entering Tilbury Dock to load, straight off Everard's yard at Greenhithe. The last of her sides had been sheathed to double them. Her high bulwarks (rails to bargemen) were held in place with steel plates bolted together. This major refit cannot have been a truly commercial decision as the age of sail was well and truly over. The only rivals 'as the last sailing barges' were those supplying the mills at Ipswich with grain from the Royal Docks in London, but the number of cargoes were getting less and less. The Ipswich millers Cranfield Bros still had the fully rigged *Spinaway C*, but she was only used for lightering until being sold in 1967. After this the *Cambria* was the only barge trading under sail and in spite of her dogged skippers absolute determination to carry on under sail it was obvious that the barge could not continue for much longer.

On one occasion the *Cambria* was coming away from Green's Mill, Maldon where she had been with wheat and was unable to tack out, because the council had put yacht moorings in the river. A launch went to her rescue below Cook's yard and towed her a little way down the River Blackwater so that she could continue on her passage to London.

In 1956 I remember the excitement on *Xylonite* when we saw the *Cambria*, with her bowsprit down and everything set, going past Southend.

bound 'up and along' towards Yarmouth. It was a brisk winter's day and she made a most romantic sight heading off into the dusk towards the Swin, a narrow channel between sandbanks.

When we came to anchor in the Lower Hope, Gordon Hardy skipper of the *Portlight* shouted across 'did you see the *Cambria*? That was real barging!'

The crews on the remaining nine barges still carrying cargoes under sail, were mostly trading to Mistley and Ipswich, and seldom met Bob Roberts. He was surprisingly unsympathetic to these young men who had a great desire to keep sailing barges going as long as possible.

A few years later Paddy O'Driscoll, mate on one of the motor barges, recalls 'I can remember towing him (Bob) out of the dock a couple of times. He tended to think that motor bargemen were an inferior species, but with a living to earn, it was necessary to have an engine.' Paddy went on 'we never really got to know him. Some skippers spoke disparagingly of his book writing activities. I remember one saying 'he's down below, with his typewriter running hot.'

The sailing barges were forced to spend a great deal of time waiting for a favourable 'fair' wind and the crews went 'ship visiting.' Bargemen also had time to while away when waiting to be loaded, which sometimes took days in the London Docks. This resulted in little groups of bargemen sitting in the stern cabins with cups of tea spinning tales. The sailing bargemen had had interesting working lives and perfected the art of yarning. Harold Smy, of the *Beatrice Maud*, could keep a barge's cabin or the corner of a pub, enthralled for hours. Jim Lawrence, who as a young man, at the time *Cambria* was still trading, was skipper of the *Memory*, also perfected the art of nautical 'aft cabin' yarns. After a successful career as a sail maker, charter and racing barge skipper, Jim can still bring an audience almost to tears of laughter with his dry bargemen's tales, always with a twist at the end.

What Bob Roberts did, with his training in journalism, was to take bargemen's tales and turn them into books. The other bargemen thought that this was almost a betrayal of their occupation and they called him the 'Boasting Barge Master,' a play on the title of his first, and possibly best, book. It was unfair, he was just trying to tell the bargeman's story, but success certainly breeds jealousy. However thirty years after his death many of Bob's books are still in print, which is good going.

The hard winter of 1962-63 affected the *Cambria's* earnings. On January 1 the barge had orders to load 100tons of ground-nut extract in London for Great Yarmouth. For this trip Robert Daws joined her as fourth hand, having travelled by train through the snow from Cambridge. His father was a friend of Bob Roberts and they had received a card from Bob saying that for his sixteenth birthday Robert could have a trip on the barge.

The hard winter had already started when Robert Daws joined the barge at Yarmouth in December 1962. On the passage down the coast it was almost warmer than being ashore, but after they had anchored for the night, off Grays, they found the wheel was just a disc of frozen snow. Robert made several other trips, once 'borrowing' coal from Everard's lighters off Greenhithe and another time 'collecting' abandoned cargo slings in Tilbury Docks to sell in Yarmouth, both normal barging practices which might not have been entirely within the law.

In the freezing weather in 1963 the *Cambria* was loaded with groundnut on January 10 at Tilbury and then sailed down to Greenhithe where ice, wind and snow kept her weather bound until January 14. She reached Harwich on January 27, but was again weather bound by ice floes, snow and easterly gales, but she finally reach Yarmouth on February 3. She was back in London on February 20 and loaded 80tons of pulp for Dover, but had to call at Greenhithe for repairs and reached Dover on February 26.

In March she took 100tons of maize to

The *Cambria* in the Royal Docks, London, May 23 1969. The barge had brought 122tons of malt from R&W Pauls, Ipswich to load on to the *SS City of Exeter*. As malt was very bulky and light the barge is not very deep in the water

Yarmouth and another 102tons of groundnut expeller to Yarmouth again. In April 20 she loaded 50tons of bone meal and 50tons of 'horse and hoof' to Cliff Quay, Ipswich. So in three months she had carried just five freights, mostly well below her capacity. On May 1 she went on Everard's yard at Greenhithe and Bob began overseeing a major refit that included refastening and sheathing the outside of the hull with another layer of planks. She was here for five months and left the yard on October 1. The sheathing may have been due to ice in the previous winter as many wooden barges received a lot of waterline damage that winter.

In February 1964 Philip 'Ginger' Latham joined Bob as mate on the *Cambria* when the barge was mostly trading outside the Thames Estuary, sometimes to Great Yarmouth. On one trip the *Cambria* anchored off Harwich, waiting for the tide to get in the harbour. When they came to get the anchor up it had fouled on something on the bottom. Three of them, Bob, Ginger and Robert Daws, on the windlass had 'gut wrenching' hard work to get the anchor up to water level and they lifted the stern out of the water. They found that the anchor had picked up three underwater cables.

'I thought they had moved them' said Bob, a bit surprised at the discovery. Ginger and Robert Daws stood aft of the mast as Bob slipped the cable and the barge bucked like a rocking horse. Robert remembers Bob as being an extremely good seaman, but very intolerant of anyone who got something wrong.

During the four and a quarter years Philip Latham was in the *Cambria* she visited Dunkirk twice, once to commemorate the evacuation and liberation of the port and once when a storm drove her there. Although the *Cambria* had not been to the 1940 Dunkirk Evacuation, Everards decided to send her there in 1965, on the twenty-fifth anniversary of the evacuation, to represent their barges that had been there. Everard's barges *Ethel Everard* and *Royalty* had been lost there. The *Ethel Everard* had been towed across to France loaded with food and drinking water and was beached four miles south of Dunkirk at La Panne. She had to be left there but the Germans re-floated her later and used her as a coal hulk. The *Royalty* had also been towed across with ammunition and was ordered to beach so that it could be unloaded as quickly as possible. However the situation deteriorated rapidly as she was bombed and machine-gunned from the air. Captain H Miller and his crew abandoned the barge and managed to return to England on a tug.

On the 1965 visit to Dunkirk the barge arrived there on June 4, left on June 7 and was back in London by June 9. On this Dunkirk Evacuation revisit the guard ship escorting the fleet was HMS *Pellew*. Richard Weekes was serving on board HMS *Pellew*. He had met Bob Roberts before at Queenborough, when the *Cambria* was sheltering on a coastal passage. Richard invited Bob aboard HMS *Pellew* and he arrived on the mess deck with his melodeon and soon the rum and beer were flowing and a full-scale singsong was underway. Other ships heard about this and invited Bob aboard to sing, but didn't ask the crew of the *Pellew*. Because his new found friends were not invited, Bob refused to go and stayed loyally on board HMS *Pellew*.

On the second occasion the *Cambria* visited Dunkirk she was driven there by a storm. On November 29, 1965 the *Cambria* had discharged wheat at Norwich and had then received orders to go to the Victoria Dock, London to load 150tons of cattle cake. The barge was towed down to Great Yarmouth and began the passage south down the coast towards the Thames, even though the weather was very unsettled. At sea the wind was West-North-West and increased to gale force. The barge made good progress south, but off Southwold, although it was still in the afternoon, the sky went so black that there was little light. At the same time the wind increased to storm force 10. The mainsail, which was an old one, split into little pieces. The wind then backed into the south-west, driving the now helpless *Cambria* away from the coast.

Bob had a passenger aboard, who was probably a member of the Erith Sailing Club, of which he was an honorary member. He called him up to help, but he was too seasick to help steer the barge in the huge seas. The *Cambria* was driven past the Galloper and out into the North Sea. She would not have survived the gale unless she had been a very good sea boat with a good crew and had had that major refit two years before.

At daylight Bob and his mate 'Ginger' Latham recognized the grey steel works at Dunkirk. It was still blowing a northwest gale, but the barge entered Dunkirk under reduced sail and anchored off the lock gates. Everards sent out another mainsail by 'return of post' and had another new one made. The *Cambria* sailed from Dunkirk on December 12, loaded 150 tons of groundnut on December 21 and arrived back in Great Yarmouth on December 23.

Richard Weekes met Bob Roberts again at Queenborough in 1966, between March 14-25. The BBC had chartered the *Cambria* for a television series called 'King of the River'. In this series, a character called 'Jos King' played a Bob Roberts type barge skipper. Bob was very happy about the fee the barge was receiving, but had fallen out with the star of the series.'

The BBC was attracted to the *Cambria* and her skipper because she was the last vessel trading under sail in northern Europe. As a young man Bob had sailed on the brigantine *Waterwitch* with Captain C. H. Deacon. He was very well aware that Deacon, master of the last brigantine, and Captain Will Cort, of Par, master of the *Katie*, the last tops'l schooner without an engine, had become national figures in the interwar years.

Although the press loved him Bob's out-spoken habits didn't endure him to many of his fellow bargemen. Once Hervey Benham was amazed when on trip with Bob and the Ipswich motor barges would not give him a 'pluck'(tow) down the River Orwell and went across to the other side the river to avoid him. That broke one of the unwritten codes of the coast as bargemen always helped each other.

In the final years of sail on the East Coast sailing barges relied on the occasional tow to remain a commercial proposition. Once the *Cambria* was becalmed off Harwich with a cargo bound for Ipswich. An Ipswich tug skipper spotted the becalmed barge and gave her a tow up the Orwell. Following the traditional practices, at Ipswich, Bob boarded the tug to thank the skipper and dropped a tip into the skipper's hand and said very generously ' buy all the boys a drink.' This turned out to be a modest five shillings and might have bought the skipper a drink. That tug skipper didn't offer the *Cambria* a tow again.

The hard facts of economics were hitting Bob's dream of going on trading under sail. He told friends that the barge simply was not making enough cash to maintain the aging hull.

Many people on the coast had a soft spot for sail, as most of them had started in sailing barges. There was a great deal of good will directed towards the *Cambria* and her now famous skipper, but it was not always returned. The truth was that Bob was basically a loner, happily turning his barge up the coast in a fresh breeze. Although he did have very loyal friends, he was not at all at ease with media people and at times with his fellow bargemen.

In 1967 I was walking along Ipswich Dock when I met Bob coming ashore from the *Cambria*. We got into conversation and he was interested in how I got my first little book published. It started to rain and he asked me down into the barge's foc's'le to talk about it. I asked him why he kept on working under sail when he could have earned a good income on one of Everards coastal vessels. He looked at me very hard and said 'I will tell you this, I earn nothing out of all this television work.'

During this period another film was made about a passage from London to Lowestoft. As there was only a skipper and mate aboard at this stage the cameraman slept in the fo'c'sle and the producer Anna Pavord slept in the spare berth aft.

The *Cambria* was still being fixed to take

The *Cambria* below Woolwich on March 9 1969 The barge had left Rochford and sailed light to collect 140tons of fruit juice from *SS Athenian* in the West India Dock. In the trading days barges almost always 'picked up' their bowsprits when they got in the rivers

cargoes to Great Yarmouth, to J. & H. Bunn, who had a wharf opposite the Town Hall, although sometimes *Cambria* was discharged into lorries at the Town Quay for Bunn's. The barge also went to the millers J. Lee-Barber & Co who had a river berth above the road bridge at Yarmouth.

Yarmouth was notorious amongst bargemen for its difficult entrance, both for its steep seas and dangerous eddy in the entrance. Bob Roberts considered that the only feasible time to enter Yarmouth under sail was shortly after high water. For the first hour of ebb there was a gently eddy and this acted as a 'brake,' slowing down the barge around Bush Bend. Several motor coasters had gone up the harbour on the flood and 'kissed' the shore even with an anchor down. During this period Bob Roberts made his hundredth passage in and out of Yarmouth, which was a considerable achievement.

On passage the barge kept sailing all the time, if the wind was fresh and favourable. If not, she sailed with a 'fair' tide and then anchored until the tide was favourable. I remember seeing the lonely brown sails of the *Cambria* tacking through Hollesley Bay in this period and on another occasion on a windless day she was anchored out near the Cutler Bank. By

P.L.A. Nº 1

CAM

then there were charter barges making passages on the East Coast, but *Cambria* was the only barge under way in the winter and the only one still carrying cargoes.

The time had come for Everard to part with their last barge. The records show that on February 2, 1966 the ownership of the *Cambria* passed from Everards to Alfred William Roberts. The only detail available is that Bob had bought the barge under a 'special arrangement'. Michael Everard, who was later head of the company, said that they had given Bob the barge, by way of a thank you for all the years he had done with the firm. Everards became Bob's agent fixing his freights and generally managing the barge.

Bob then hoisted his seagull 'bob' (house flag) to replace Everards well known red and white company house flag, but it was not quite the same. There had been a rule in Everards that if any of the coasters met any of their sailing barges at sea they had to give them a tow, if needed. The first time *Cambria* was fixed to do freight to Norwich, Bob found one of Everard's coasters at Great Yarmouth and asked to be towed up there. Later he got a bill from Everards and Bob, never a man to suffer in silence, was absolutely furious that his old firm had charged him. For a few weeks it was the talk of the coast that Bob was angry at being charged for a tow.

In 1967 the *Cambria* was lying on the Hard at Pin Mill, near to where Bob Roberts lived, in the hamlet beside the stream. Apparently some of her cargo, possibly fish meal, had got wet and smelt very strongly. This did not please many of the residents of Pin Mill. However most people were pleased when Bob returned home because it usually meant

that he was in the 'Butt and Oyster' singing and playing his accordion and generally putting the world to right.

On Yarmouth quay holiday makers often came down to admire the last sailing barge carrying cargoes coming in under sail, but they seldom understood what she was. Questions such as 'did you come down from London by canal' infuriated Bob, but when they asked him how he saw the land in the dark he had a ready reply. His dog smelt the land. In fact Bob was extremly good at coastal navigation, but the *Cambria* did have a good sea dog.

The dog carried on the *Cambria* at this stage was Dusty, a very intelligent 'Suffolk lurcher' bitch, third in the line from her grandmother to be carried aboard the barge. When the barge 'winded' (tacked) Dusty used to move from her nest on one side of the skylight around to the new windward side. At one stage she had pups and one of these was the 'barge hound' Stormy. (Bob was renowned for singing the shanty 'Stormy Weather Boys'). Stormy was owned by the barge skipper Peter Light and could walk slowly up and down ladders by putting her legs through the rungs.

Philip Latham stayed on the barge until July 1968 but stayed with Everards for a further twenty-three years and became a master in their motor coasters. Phillip claims that he 'started work in the nineteenth century.' The whole way that the barge was sailed was completely Victorian, without an engine there was no other way of doing it.

In 1968 Bob Roberts went to Crescent Shipping, the Medway firm who then had most of the remaining barges trading around the Thames Estuary, and said that Everards could no longer find him freights. This was no doubt true, Everards had moved into oil tankers and far larger short sea vessels. Bob received a warm welcome from Crescent Shipping because it was being run by Tony Winter. He had left school in the mid-1950s and gone into sailing barges and had become mate on Crescent's *Thyra*, an auxiliary barge trading with wheat between

The *Cambria* discharging cattle cake from Tilbury at the Eastern Counties Farmers wharf, Ipswich Dock in 1970. When I stopped and took this photograph there was no sign this would be the last commercial cargo delivered by sail in Britain.

Hull and Peterborough. After this Tony went into the office and also rigged out the wooden sailing barge *Lord Roberts* for charter work.

In fact Ray Sully, a barge owner, who had gone in with Crescent Shipping was managing the London office and fixed most of the *Cambria's* freights at ten per cent commission. In about 1969 the *Cambria* was up at Green's mill Maldon. After discharging wheat, Bob Roberts wanted to go home for Christmas, but the barge needed pumping out every day. Barry Pearce said he would keep an eye on her. The instructions on how to use the motor pump took the form of a rhyme left under the binnacle cover. By this time Barry believed, there must have been many people on the East Coast who knew that rhyme.

For two years Tony Winter did everything in his power to find freights for *Cambria* to help Bob live his dream of continuing to trade under sail. In her final years the *Cambria* was sailed by two people, there was no money to pay for a third hand, but Bob often took along a passenger, who was expected to give a helping hand with the heavy anchor work and sail handling. Bob had a job getting a crew and once Richard Duke of Pin Mill did a trip to help him out. Dick Durham joined the barge on Pin Mill Hard and was mate for the last nine months and went on to become a yachting journalist and author.

Bob had become a regular figure in the folk singing circuit and was the subject of magazine articles and the BBC made two documentaries for national television. The handsome *Cambria* took on the status of the '*Cutty Sark* of the narrow seas' and her outspoken master became a national figure.

In 1970 Richard Weekes was mate on the motor barge *Phoenician*, a former sailing barge. They often came across the *Cambria*, which by then was spending a lot of time lying on the buoys in the Thames and was carrying a motor pump because of a problem with leaks. This didn't stop Bob and his mate from enjoying evenings ashore in the 'Theobalds Arms' in Grays.

Once the *Cambria* took a cargo of soya bean meal to Lee Barber's at Lowestoft. John Lee Barber was on the phone to the Crescent Shipping office to say 10tons of the cargo was wet and they couldn't, even though the barge was lovely, have that happen again.

The leaks were becoming a real problem and Bob didn't have the money to do major repairs. It appears to have been the barge's insurers who decided that the *Cambria* should stay in the Thames Estuary and no longer go to Lowestoft or Yarmouth. I learnt about this and reported it in my *Sea Breezes* 'Sail Review' feature which resulted in the magazine office receiving an explosive phone call from Bob Roberts threatening to sue the magazine. I heard that *Cambria* was on passage to Ipswich and, as it was a Saturday morning, I went down to the lock just as the brown sails of the *Cambria* came ghosting up the river past Cliff Quay. I borrowed a barge's boat off one of the Ipswich barges on the Dock End yard and sculled out to *Cambria* as Bob Roberts and Dick Durham picked up the buoy off the lock.

Bob seemed surprised when I climbed aboard, it took quite a brave man to step on *Cambria*! When I explained why I was there Bob roared 'if any of those clerks in the office read that I will loose freights and money!'

I pointed out that the clerks in the office would know all about it already and Bob realised at once that my information had come from an agent's office. 'Just tell me the name of who ever told you' thundered Bob ' and I will soon put him right!' I though it best not to reveal the name of my informant.

Some companies were happy to have the *Cambria* deliver freights because they knew it would appear in the local paper and bring them publicity. The barge regularly took wheat to Green's Mill at Maldon, where a barge under sail was still considered to be perfectly normal. In the old days the upper River Blackwater was clear of yacht moorings, but getting up there under sail became increasingly difficult.

Another time the *Cambria* went to the oil refinery on the Isle of Grain to collect 70tons of high grade lubricating oil in barrels for export from a ship in the London Docks. It was not long before Mr Wright at the Isle of Grain was on the phone to Tony Winter in Crescent's office at Strood. 'This barge you have sent us is lovely and the skipper is really good, but we have had her here before and the crane keeps getting mixed up in the brails and its taking a long time to load. Don't send her here again.' Tony Winter broke the sad news to Bob Roberts that they could not longer find him freights.

In the autumn of 1970 Derek Lawrence organized a £30 sub from Cory Bros for Bob to pay his bills. The *Cambria* did take another freight, a cargo of 100tons of groundnut from Tilbury to Ipswich. As there was a head wind in Ipswich Dock, Bob and his mate had to winch the barge on a dolly line from the lock gates up to the Eastern Countries Farmer's wharf. The groundnut was loaded into lorries and taken up the road for storage. This was the last real commercial cargo delivered under sail in northern Europe. Bob Roberts wrote a letter to the *East Anglian Daily Times*, thanking everyone for helping him to keep going under sail for so long. She had no rivals for her place in history since it was several years since the last Ipswich barge had carried a cargo under sail, only a few hookers on the west coast of Ireland were carrying turf.

Bob also made his final entry in his cargo book, just a simple notebook he had kept. The first entry was on October 29 1954 and it ended on October 22 1970 with the passage from Ipswich 'to London.' They left at 3am and arrived at 5pm. Bob's final entry is 'barge now out of commission.'

Perhaps the most surprising thing was that Bob, after sixteen years in the *Cambria*, and raging against motor ships, that he went off and bought one. He sold the *Cambria* to the newly formed Maritime Trust and bought the 260ton *Vectis Isle* and moved off to the Isle of Wight. He never wrote or spoke in public about his seven years as the master of a motor vessel and took very little interest in *Cambria's* new role.

On April 20 1971 the Maritime Trust held a major Press Conference aboard the *Wellington*, the headquarters of the Honourable Company of Master Mariners, on the Embankment in London. The Maritime Trust were appealing for £2million to restore *H.M.S. Warrior*, *H.M.S Gannett* and a huge assortment of craft from all over the British Isles. This was a major initiative to save the nation's past.

The *Cambria*, newly painted up and under the new Maritime Trust's house flag, was sailed up by Bob Roberts to Tower Pier outside the Tower of London. Bob told us on the quay how pleased he was that the Maritime Trust had bought his barge to save her for the nation. He said how he hated the idea of his barge becoming a charter barge and being sailed for pleasure. Also, Bob, true to form, was a bit sceptical about the Trust's long-term ability to save the barge. The Trust for their part was much more up beat and said over the next seven years they intended to spend £35,000 on restoring the *Cambria*. In 1971 this was a considerable sum of money.

It was one thing to have a wonderful idea to save many of the nation's historic ships, but it was quite another to achieve it. The *Cambria* was taken to Rochester and berthed at a quay so that the paying public could go aboard her and look at a good exhibition of barge photographs in the hold. This should have been a perfect future, but it didn't work and her role as a static 'historic ship' was a fatal mistake. When a vessel goes to sea she has to be well maintained or she will sink, but a vessel tied up to a quay can remain afloat for years with no real maintenance.

That is what happened to *Cambria*, down on the Medway where the barge remained tied to the quay while other sailing barges were out racing and sailing in the estuary. The *Cambria* was doomed.

The tiller steered barge *Cygnet* passing the barge blocks and the 'Butt & Oyster' at Pin Mill, on the River Orwell. The *Cambria's* home port during her final trading days.

The Cambria Trust committee celebrating the award of a Heritage Lottery Grant on *Cambria* at Sheerness, in March, 2007. Tony Ellis, second from the right

Chapter Three / INTO THE SECOND CENTURY

The Maritime Trust moved the *Cambria* to St Katharine's Dock, London to be part of their Historic Ship Collection. St Katharine's, next to the Tower of London, is one of Britain's most popular tourist centres and it seemed to be a good place to have ships on display and open to the public, but the revenue never met the huge expense of keeping up these elderly vessels. I remember visiting *Cambria* in about 1980 and there was the unmistakeable smell of rotten wood below decks and there was moss growing on the decks in the seams of the planking. Worse still no proper maintenance was taking place. A ship tied up to a quay 'for ever' looses its soul.

The Maritime Trust, although its intentions were always honourable, reached a point where they just wanted to cut and run. They were desperate to get rid of their huge fleet of historic and decaying vessels. In January 1987 *Cambria* was towed from St Katherine's Dock down to a muddy creek off The Swale in north Kent. Here she was berthed at Sittingbourne at the lower end of the tiny creek at The Dolphin Barge Yard Museum. A year later The Cambria Restoration Project was formed to save the *Cambria* and they confidently predicted that for some £100,000 she would return to sail again. The hold was in a dreadful mess, but when the barge went on the blocks it was believed that the hull was in reasonable order. The Project pulled up the covering board and undertook some minor repairs.

The Dolphin Barge Museum, a former brick works barge yard, on Milton Creek was the brainchild of Tony Ellis who had, in his own quiet way, steered the museum through its early stages. Tony then became Project Leader of The Cambria Restoration Project, but for ten years the *Cambria* lay at Sittingbourne, basically rotting away. I have nothing but admiration for the loyal band of enthusiasts who plugged away for years to keep the *Cambria* project alive

Tony Ellis became chairman of the new Cambria Trust and in 1996 paid the Maritime Trust one pound for the barge at a ceremony at the Dolphin Barge Yard. Tony had been searching around for helpers to get the *Cambria* restoration project going and approached Geoff Collard. Geoff had spent seven years on the River Thames in the 1930s as an apprentice Waterman and some of his time was used training on sailing barges. Later he became Managing Director of the Tate & Lyle river operations, which by 1964 included the sailing barge *May* recently purchased from Cranfields of Ipswich. Geoff had done a tremendous amount of work helping to save other barges and while commodore of the Thames Barge Sailing Club he negotiated the purchase of the barge *Pudge* from Crescent Shipping. However, Geoff was now retired, and as his wife had said that he was not to get involved in any more barge projects, he suggested that his son William should become involved. William Collard was just the person for this project because he had already been involved in shipbuilding and repair on the Medway and Thames. He had worked for Crescent Shipping at their Rochester barge yard in the 1960s where he assisted in the design of several new build powered coastal vessels. However, the company still had a large fleet of wooden motor barges which were mostly old cut down sailing barges and William was able to learn a lot about wooden barge construction during this period.

By 1996 William was working for the waste management company Cleanaway that had its own rubbish barge fleet. This operation was managed by a Thames waterman friend, David Allen, and he persuaded the Directors to give the Cambria Trust a redundant barge for

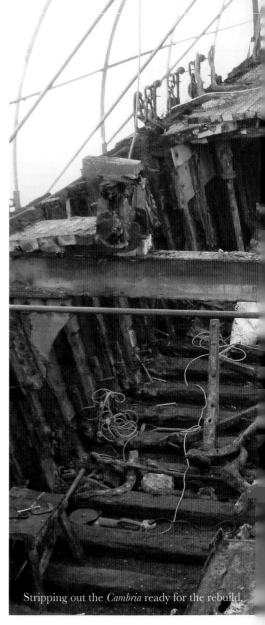

Stripping out the *Cambria* ready for the rebuild.

conversion into a dry-dock. Without this gift the *Cambria* would not have been saved.

The Cleanaway barge was the *Barbara Jean* that fortunately had an aluminium rollup hatch. Because aluminium scrap value was high William was able to give the hatch to a metal dealer, and in return he cut down the sides of the lighter to make a dry dock for the *Cambria* to float into. Frank Spice was an unofficial harbour master at the Dolphin yard and he took on the task of getting the *Cambria* afloat. Basically the *Cambria's* bow and stern

were beginning to fall apart from the hull and Frank had to carry about a ton and a half of cement in buckets to fill up an inch and a half gap where the sides were coming away from the bottom. He also made up a steel frame to hold the stern together which was enough to get the hull to float again with pumps running.

The *Barbara Jean* was fitted with valves so that she could be filled with water. She was then towed into the middle of Milton Creek, outside the tiny Dolphin yard creek and sunk. William Collard supervised the moving of the leaking

Cambria out of the Dolphin yard and over the dry dock lighter on a very high tide. As the tide fell the barge settled comfortably into her new berth. At low tide the former rubbish barge's valves were closed and as the tide rose the new dry dock, with *Cambria* sitting inside, floated and was towed back into the Dolphin yard.

The years went quietly by, Basil Brambley, a tireless worker, joined the Trust in about 2000. The Dolphin Yard had always had trouble financing itself because people could walk down the river wall and look at the workshops

The new frames on the starboard side are oak from Somerset on the old planks, 2010.

The new steel keelson in the stern.

and barges in the creek without paying to go in. They managed to raise money to do some repairs to *Cambria*. A few forward port frames were replaced, but the barge was deteriorating faster than the work was being done so that by 2005 there was very little sound wood left in the hull.

The *Cambria* project moved very slowly forward until the day the owners of the Dolphin Barge Museum site served a notice on the Cambria Trust to quit. All the barges had to be removed. The *Oak*, a Maldon barge built in 1881 was sadly cut up, but the Cambria Trust sprang into life to save their beloved barge. The Medway Port Authority gave permission for the *Cambria* to be berthed in the outer harbour at Sheerness Dockyard. However, the Trust had not planned for a move from Dolphin and a lot of the strength of the dry dock had been removed. William considered that the vessel needed added steelwork before a six-hour tow to Sheerness could be contemplated. Funds were very limited but a sudden contribution from the Port of London Authority allowed the

Rear Admiral Bruce Richardson talking to master shipwright Tim Goldsack on *Cambria*, 2009

Things were really starting to move forward. The Collard's long-standing connection to the Company of Watermen and Lightermen of the River Thames also started to bring much-needed good will to the project.

A small Cambria Trust meeting held at 'The Three Daws', Gravesend, a pub with a long association with the Thames tideway, in the winter of 2007 was very up beat. It had been hinted to the Trust that they would be awarded a Heritage Lottery Fund grant. Without it the *Cambria* had no real future beyond being dumped on the saltings of the River Medway which would have been an ignoble end to one of the finest wooden sailing barges ever built. The good news was that a Heritage Lottery Fund grant of £990.000 was awarded towards the rebuild and the Cambria Trust had to raise the rest of the money for the total rebuild.

The original plan had been to totally rebuild the *Cambria* in one of the dry docks in The Camber at Sheerness. The Medway Ports Authority had agreed to this, but then decided that they would apply for their own heritage grant to have this dock restored. So that on September 1, 2007 the *Cambria* was moved to Faversham in her dry dock. The tow took about six hours, with a Medway Ports launch going in front with a blue light flashing. Over 150 people watched the barge arrive at Faversham. This was also the time of the Faversham Hop Festival and the Deputy Mayor of the Swale Council was there to hand over a wreath of hop vines which were used to decorate the barge's bows. A folk dancing group performed on the quay and someone played 'Rule Britannia' on a violin. Faversham was very pleased to welcome the *Cambria* for her rebirth.

On the more practical side Colin Frake and Brian Pain had offered the barge in her dry dock a berth on Standard Quay. The mooring ropes secured the dry dock to the quay and there was endless background organization to prepare for the rebuild. William Collard had to resign as a Trustee so that he could take up the full time role of Project Manager as required by

necessary strengthening work to be completed and in April 2006 the successful move to Sheerness took place.

Initial meetings with the Heritage Lottery Fund had indicated that an application for funds would be favourably considered, so Tony Ellis commenced filling in the massive form almost on his own. Rear Admiral Bruce Richardson, who had commanded naval ships and been the Chief Harbour Master for the Port of London became Patron, bringing with him good contacts from the Port of London.

Looking forward on the new deck, 2010

The shipwrights Geoff 'Frog' Ingle, Ryan Dale and Jon Hall with Tim Goldsack waiting for *Cambria* to re-float after her total re-build, March 2011.

CAMBRIA

Re-launching the *Cambria* at Faversham, 2011.

The Cambria Trust's volunteers acted as guides to the public during the rebuild and helped paint the barge.

HLF. Contracts had to be drawn up with Tim Goldsack, for him to undertake the rebuilding of the barge in three years and the Trust had to assure the Lottery monitor, Jason Lowe, that they could manage this major project competently.

Work preparing the dry dock for the rebuild went on until December. To increase the space, walkways were built on either side, and then a cover fitted so that the shipwrights could work in the dry. Tim Goldsack and his team of Faversham shipwrights had previously rebuilt the 44ft smack *Emmeline* and refitted his own steel sailing barge *Decima*. Their previous job had been the total rebuild of the 82ft wooden barge *Dawn*, also funded by a Heritage Lottery Grant, at Heybridge. Again she had been in a dry dock, but there was endless work carrying every piece of timber aboard over a river wall. This time, with the far larger *Cambria*, they made a slot in the roof of the cover so that timber could be craned in. A public viewing

gallery was also built and in time a Heritage Centre was opened on the quay to help visitors understand the history of barges.

Cambria Trust volunteers cleared out the barge's hold and then the shipwrights started stripping out the rotten wood. In January, 2008 William Collard decided to removed the heavily corroded 24x8 inch RSJ steel keelson with riveted fish plates, basically the back bone of the barge, and replace it with a smaller stronger steel keelson. The bottom had been sheathed on the inside when the barge was built and this was removed to find the 3" wooden bottom was 'almost as good as new,' but another layer of planks was added. This was the only part of the old hull to be kept. Six shipwrights worked in two teams, starting at either end of the hold replacing the frames and floors and renewing the sheathing. Also an apprentice spent hours chipping out the cement put in the bottom, which had been put there to float her out of the Dolphin Yard twelve years before.

Richard Titchener at the wheel of *Cambria* in the Thames Match 2011.

The main piece to be replaced was the steel keelson, virtually the backbone of the barge. A flat-bottomed barge does not have a keel but has a keelson inside running the length of the barge. In old age barges will 'hog', that is sag at either end. When Tim Goldsack rebuilt the barge *Dawn* he had strengthened the hull by fitting more laminated knees, but with *Cambria* he went a step further and extended the new steel keelson slightly up into the bow and stern to make the hull much stronger.

At some point during *Cambria's* long stay at Sittingbourne the steering wheel had been stolen. In 2008 local news was that the old established ships chandlers, Starbucks, at Gravesend was closing, and there was a barge's wheel hung outside for sale. William Collard and Basil Brambley set off and purchased the wheel for *Cambria*.

After one year of work by Tim Goldsack and his shipwrights most of the frames and timbers on the floor had been replaced. Some forty oak

trees, kindly given by Mrs Angela Yeoman from her estate near Frome in Somerset, had been used. The trees were about two hundred years old, and the area was replanted with new oak.

Brian Pain lent the Trust a lovely old clapboard building on Standard Quay to became a Visitors Centre and Meeting Room. The Cambria Trust became the catalyst for starting an apprentice scheme for four young shipwrights to be trained for two years. Some worked on the *Cambria* and others were helping to rebuild the Scottish wooden trawler *Morayshire* and the barge *Lady of the Lea*.

On November 25, 2008 Tony Ellis, chairman of the Cambria Trust, died of a stroke, age 63 This was heart breaking for his family and everyone in the Trust were tremendously shocked and sad that its founder had, after twenty years of hard work, not lived to see the rebuilding project completed.

As a young man Tony had travelled around the Thames Estuary on his motorbike recording

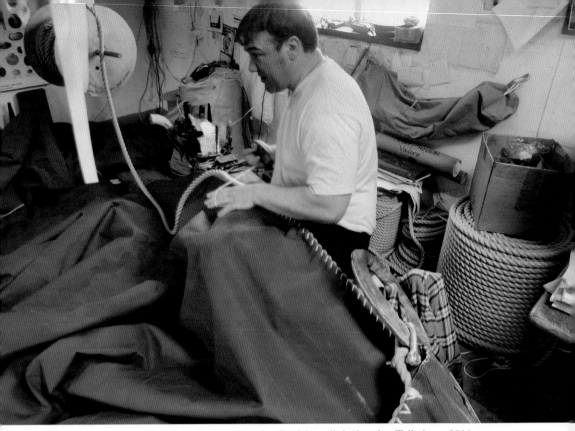

The traditional sailmaker Steve Hall making the *Cambria's* sails by hand at Tollesbury, 2011.

the fast diminishing trading barges, an interest which subsequently allowed him to publish his own book 'The Sailing Barges of Maritime England.' He was a founder member of the Society for Spritsail Barge Research and the first secretary of the Sailing Barge Association. He had also been editor of the magazine 'The Thames Guardian', published by the River Thames Society. His knowledge of the River Thames and the vessels that plied their trade was to be sorely missed and he was a great loss to the *Cambria* restoration project.

Bruce Richardson volunteered to take on a more active role and was appointed Chairman of the Trustees. He vacated his position of Patron and actor David Suchet was asked to take over this role, to which he readily agreed. David lived by the Thames and owned a Dutch barge, and was a member of the Watermen's company, so was maritime minded.

During the winter of 2008-9 the main problem with the rebuild was the shape of the bows. At one stage during the long years at Sittingbourne *Cambria* started to float on the tide, but gradually filled with water and had then sunk. The hull went out of shape and the bows, particularly the starboard side, altered. Although both ends of the hull had been jacked up 9" to take the hog out (the bow and the stern sagged down), finding the deck line 'sheer' (upward curve) of the bow was difficult to fix. Going back to basics, Tim and William fastened thin strips of timber called spiles onto the hull and moved them up and down until they were happy that the hull shape could be returned to her original lines. They were using their eyes rather than dimensions from drawings.

By the early summer of 2010 the deck was on and the hull nearly planked up on the outside and once again she was starting to be a really strong barge with a long future ahead. The original winches were sent away, to be restored, and new spars were made. The original main mast was wooden, but a new steel

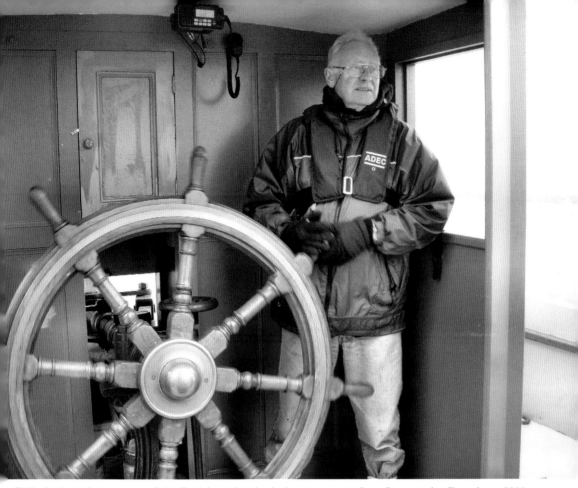

Philip Latham, former mate of the *Cambria*, at the wheel when on passage from Gravesend to Faversham, 2011.

mast was made. Only the 'headstick' for the tops'l remains from the old barge. Originally it had been planned to have the traditional flat wooden leeboards, which were very practical for working in docks, but since it was planned to race the *Cambria*, new 22ft hollow steel shaped leeboards were made up by Tim's work force in the adjoining Iron Wharf Yard.

In the trading days iron leeboards were tried, but the flat wooden ones were found more practical in the docks. In 1955, in the final years of the Champion Class barge racing, shaped Dutch leeboards, rather like botter's leeboards, were fitted on the *Sirdar* with great success. Later new wooden leeboards from Holland were fitted on the *Mirosa* and Alan Reekie decided to improve on these. He made hollow steel aerofoil leeboards at the Iron Wharf and fitted them on his barge *Ironsides* with such success that she was

a top racing barge between 1976-85.

In September 2010 Tim's shipwrights put on the last planks in *Cambria's* new hull while Bruce Richardson, William Collard and others were constantly looking ahead to the days when *Cambria* would have to earn her keep. The Cambria Trust would have to work hard to find the finances to keep her sailing. In some way she would have to enter the highly competitive charter business. Most people imaged that when the *Cambria* was totally rebuilt she would be fitted with an engine. The barge had been the last working sailing commercial vessel in the northern Europe and it seemed inappropriate to fit one.

The barges *Mirosa* and *Edme*, like the *Cambria*, had never had an engine, and both undertake passenger trips, but it is a great deal more difficult without an engine. The world had

The *Cambria* was first around the outer mark in the Thames Sailing Barge Match, 2011.

The *Cambria* in the Sea Reach coming up to be the first barge to finish in the 2011 Thames Barge Match.

CAMBRIA LONDON

The *Cambria* first over the finishing line off Gravesend in the Thames Match 2011.

changed since *Cambria* was built in 1906, and by 2011 charterers were expecting a barge to run to a timetable, and arrive at an agreed time.

It had been planned to build a traditional wooden barge's boat for *Cambria*, but towards the end of the rebuild finances were getting very tight. The traditional all-purpose wooden barge's boat was kept aft, in davits, on the starboard quarter, and these were about 14ft 6ins long. For the *Cambria* a 16ft grp boat was found which fitted the bill. This boat had been built in 1992 and the Thames River Police had rowed her around the British Isles and Ireland, so there was no doubt of her seaworthiness. Although a bit larger than normal, it was thought she would be suitable for young people to row around in.

Years before, when *Cambria* was a rotting hulk at Sittingbourne, the panelled skipper's stern cabin had been taken out of her and stored in a container. By November 2010 the panelling was at Faversham being fitted into the new hull by Basil and a number of other volunteers. Barry Pearce, the Maldon authority on barges, had pointed out that the *Cambria's* name on her stern was 'wrong.' He sent photographs showing the original name carving that had followed the Everard style of having the first letters of *Cambria* and London carved larger that the rest of letters. Another transom had been boarded over the original carving, probably in the 1963 rebuild. I passed Barry's photographs on to William Collard, but when the new stern came to be built these had been 'mislaid.' A bit of rushing about and the information was found again and the *Cambria's* name reverted to its original lay out. Little details like this helped to keep the whole restoration accurate.

After £1.4m and three and a half years of work by Tim Goldsack and his shipwrights, and a considerable amount of work and painting by the Cambria Trust's excellent volunteers, the great day came when the barge was re-launched. On March 21 2011 the morning was bright and sunny when the stopcocks on the dry dock were opened to allow it to fill with water. As the shipwrights, William Collard and Bruce Richardson paced about restlessly on the barge's deck the tide crept up over the mud of Faversham Creek and the crowd on the quay and opposite bank grew larger.

As the barge finally rose with the tide and moved, the school children on the opposite bank, who had been following the rebuild, screamed with excitement. The workboat men of the creek took the event more calmly and the lines from the small tugs *Pep* and *Joker* were put on the *Cambria*. She was towed out into the creek and down to the Iron Wharf. Here, to everyone's delight, the new hull made very little water. She must have looked almost the same as when she was launched in 1906, accept the wheel-shelter was slightly higher. The theory was that men are taller than when she was originally launched.

After four months of tremendous activity at Faversham all the *Cambria's* spars were up, the standing and running rigging was in place and the new sails, made by traditional sailmaker Steve Hall of Tollesbury, arrived. The first charter was to Richard Titchener's Sea Change Trust, an organization for training young people. Richard and his team made a considerable contribution to the final stages of the rigging out. Then Richard became the skipper when the barge was towed out of from Faversham Creek in heavy rain and on July 18 new sails were set for the first time and she was sailed across the Thames Estuary to Maldon.

Three days later she was at Gravesend to take part in the 81st Thames Sailing Barge Match. In 1938 the *Cambria* had won the Coasting Class in this race and had last taken part in the Thames Sailing Barge Match race in 1955.

In 2011 on July 23 there was a fresh NW breeze for the Thames barge race, the *Cambria* ploughed out in front of the fleet. After the turning mark she was sailing at 9.3knots back up the Sea Reach to be the first barge over the finishing line off the 'Three Daws' public house at Gravesend. The *Cabby, Lady Daphne* and *Lady of the Lea* were also in this Coasting Class. At the start the Champion Bowsprit Class *Marjorie* and *Adieu* were sailing at 11.5knots down the Sea Reach and after a fast beat back from the North Oaze Buoy, Iolo Brooks' barge *Adieu* won.

That summer the *Cambria* took part in the Swale barge race with Tim Goldsack as skipper. The *Cambria* came second to the *Edme*, which is probably the fastest barge still sailing. Tim was used to sailing his 85ft steel barge *Decima*. Although used to sailing a smaller barge Tim found the *Cambria* fast and very handy when tacking up the narrow channel back to Faversham Creek, and was pleased at how well she handled. Perhaps we have the key to *Cambria's* long career and unique story of survival. Over the decades the *Cambria's* size and sailing ability made her a good earner for her owners and crews. Because of her connection to the early days of the Everard firm she was kept going longer than her commercial value dictated. Being a handsome barge inspired many people to work together to keep her afloat. All this combined to create the special magic around her. This allows *Cambria* to start another chapter in her long career.

Cambria's / PRINCIPLE DETAILS

Built in 1906 at Greenhithe by F.T Everard Traded under sail until 1970 Rebuilt 2011 at Faversham by Tim Goldsack

Hull Length 91.1ft

Beam 21.9ft

Depth 7.3ft

Gross tonnage 109 (79net)

Mainmast 49ft: topmast 43ft

Mizzen 45ft sprit 62ft

Bowsprit 38ft

Sail area 5,000 square feet.

The *Cambria* loaded 170tons for sea on a depth of 7ft 6ins, but only drew 3ft light. When sailing light the barge needed a leeboard down so that it griped the water and she could be steered.

Robert Simper sailed on some of the last barges trading under sail. Has written thirty-seven books and a regular column in the magazine *Sea Breezes* for forty-six years. Under his chairmanship he drove forward the rebuilding of the sailing barge *Dawn* and he is a Director of the Cambria Trust.

SOURCE OF ILLUSTRATIONS

Robert Daws 8 Tony Farnham 4,5,11,13 Robert Simper front cover, 3,14,28,30,36,38,40,42,45,46, 48, 50,53 Pearl Simper 31 Patricia O'Driscoll 17,18,19 William Collard 20,32,34,35,44,47 Dave Brooks back cover, the Society for Sailing Barge Research 22,25. Remainder are from the Cambria Trust collection.

Barges before the start of a race at Pin Mill